DORSET TOWN TRAILS

DORSET TOWN TRAILS

Chris Jesty

G

Roy Gasson Associates

First published in Great Britain 1985
by Roy Gasson Associates
18 Ashdene Close, Wimborne, Dorset
BH21 1TQ

Copyright © 1985 Chris Jesty

ISBN 0 948495 03 0

Printed and bound by Butler & Tanner Ltd,
London & Frome

All rights reserved

CONTENTS

Map showing the position of the towns   6

Introduction   7

Town trails (listed in alphabetical order):-

Beaminster	16-17
Blandford Forum	38-39
Bournemouth	52-58
Bridport	12-15
Christchurch	59-63
Dorchester	18-22
Lyme Regis	8-11
Poole	50-51
Shaftesbury	32-35
Sherborne	26-31
Sturminster Newton	36-37
Swanage	47-49
Wareham	44-46
Weymouth	23-25
Wimborne Minster	40-43

6

Based upon the Ordnance Survey maps with the permission of the Controller of H.M. Stationery Office.

Crown copyright reserved

SHAFTESBURY p. 32-35
SHERBORNE p. 26-31
STURMINSTER NEWTON p. 36-37
BLANDFORD FORUM p. 38-39
BEAMINSTER p. 16-17
WIMBORNE MINSTER p. 40-43
BRIDPORT p. 12-15
DORCHESTER p. 18-22
POOLE p. 50-51
CHRIST-CHURCH p. 59-63
LYME REGIS p. 8-11
WAREHAM p. 44-46
BOURNEMOUTH p. 52-58
WEYMOUTH p. 23-25
SWANAGE p. 47-49

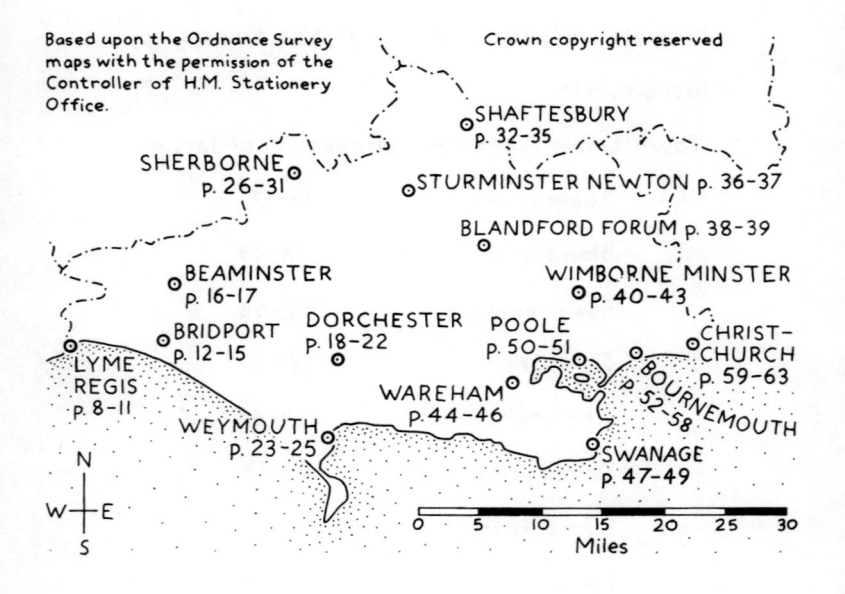

0 5 10 15 20 25 30
Miles

INTRODUCTION

Anyone who walks along the coast of Dorset will notice how the rock varies from place to place. In the towns of Dorset this geological diversity is reflected in the stone of the older buildings, from the Blue Lias of Lyme Regis to the Greensand of Shaftesbury and the Coral Rag of Sturminster Newton.

Although it is the older buildings that give the towns of Dorset their special charm, this is enhanced in many cases by sympathetic modern development. In the sections on Bridport, Wimborne and Poole I have mentioned modern buildings that harmonise with their surroundings. Other examples are Saxon Square behind the Town Hall in Christchurch, and Nightingale Court off East Street in Blandford. An example of a modern building that does not harmonise with its surroundings is that occupied by Boots the Chemists by the traffic lights in Bridport.

Because all the Dorset towns are included in this book, it is inevitable that some of the trails will be more interesting than others. The best are Sherborne, Shaftesbury and Christchurch, followed by Lyme Regis, Bridport, Dorchester, Wimborne, Swanage and Bournemouth. The towns are arranged in geographical order, roughly from west to east. All the walks return to the starting point, which is usually a car park. Most of them are about a mile long. In some cases I have suggested shorter alternatives or extensions, but I have avoided complicated routes with a lot of doubling back.

The best day to do these walks is Sunday, when the streets are quiet.

8

LYME REGIS

The charms of Lyme Regis have attracted many eminent writers to the town. Jane Austen lived in Lyme Regis in 1803 and 1804, and in her book "Persuasion" Louisa Musgrove fell down the steps called Granny's Teeth on the Cobb. Beatrix Potter stayed at Burley House in Silver Street in 1904, and used a number of Lyme Regis scenes to illustrate her books. Henry Fielding based the character of Sophie in "Tom Jones" on Sarah Andrews whom he met in the town; and John Fowles, the author of "The French Lieutenant's Woman", has lived in Lyme Regis since 1965.

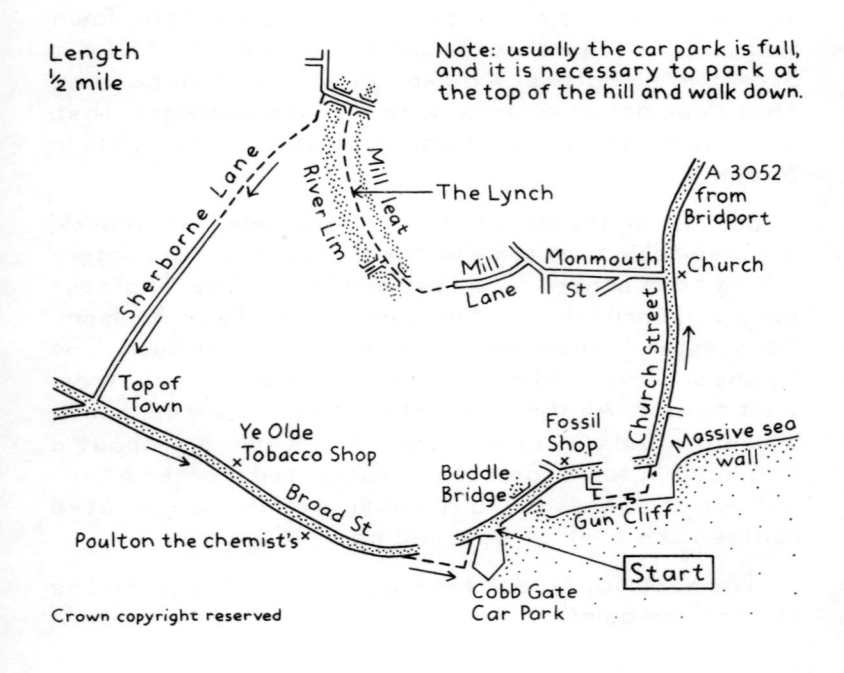

Length
½ mile

Note: usually the car park is full, and it is necessary to park at the top of the hill and walk down.

Crown copyright reserved

Lyme Regis

The trail begins at the Cobb Gate Car Park in the centre of the town. Turn right into Bridge Street and cross over the Buddle Bridge. Looking down from the right-hand parapet you can see the River Lim flowing out to sea between high stone walls. This stretch of the river is called the Buddle.

On the left is the Lyme Fossil Shop with a very fine ammonite in the window, and on the right is the Museum. Immediately past this turn right, and pass through a round-headed archway on to the Gun Cliff. Turn left, and follow the top of the sea wall, passing on the right a flight of steps which leads down to the shore in a series of twists and turns. Before leaving this area, take a look through the railings ahead at the massive sea wall on your left, and the magnificent coastal scenery in front of you.

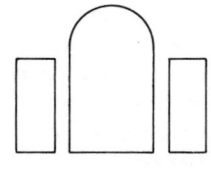

Venetian window

Leave the cliff-top by passing under a Venetian window into a covered passage. On leaving the passage, keep straight on into Church Street, which was formerly called the Butter Market. Opposite the church, turn left into Monmouth Street. Where the road forks, bear right, passing between a small triangular park and Monmouth House, where the Duke of Monmouth spent a night in 1685.

At the end of the road bear right, and then immediately turn left along the side of the Ship Inn, into Mill Lane. The River Lim makes a horseshoe bend here, coming out of one tunnel and going into another. Keep straight on up a metalled path between walls. The path crosses a mill leat, usually dry, and continues along the other side of it.

For the next two hundred yards the path runs along

a causeway called the Lynch, which separates the River Lim from the mill leat. The leat has water in it now. It is narrower than the river, and is at a higher level. Altogether this is a most attractive area, with flowers and butterflies in profusion, ducks on the leat, and occasionally a grey wagtail on the river.

At Gosling Bridge, turn left over the bridge and immediately left again, along the other side of the river. Go round a right-hand bend and climb the steep and narrow lane called Sherborne Lane, which has been here for twelve hundred years.

At the top of the hill turn left into Broad Street, now the main street of the town. On the left is the Olde Tobacco Shop where James Whistler the artist had his studio. Farther along on the right, on the side wall of Poulton the chemist's, are some photographs that were taken during the filming of "The French Lieutenant's Woman". It is fascinating to study the photographs and then go outside and compare them with the real thing. The transformation is amazing. In the photographs there are no cars. All the shop signs have been changed, and all the buildings are a different colour. What is so remarkable is that the paintwork and the shop signs look old, yet the photographs were taken in 1980.

The group of old houses in the centre of the road is called Middle Row. Keep to the right of this and you will come out onto Bell Cliff, where there is a Georgian cannon and a seat. This is where Richard Fox, the world champion town crier, stands in his tricorn hat and uniform and makes his announcements, so maintaining a tradition that goes back to 1068.

From here a flight of steps leads down to the car park.

Lyme Regis

Extension

Length ½ mile

From the Cobb Gate Car Park follow the sea front to the west. The lower road is called the Cart Road, and ends in a ramp leading down the beach. The upper road is called the Marine Parade or the Walk, and leads all the way to the Cobb. On the right is a row of beautiful pink thatched cottages in a perfect situation. The first house on the left-hand side of the road (just past Jane's Café) is Bay Cottage, the home of Captain Harville in "Persuasion". The Marine Bookshop on the right is built of Blue Lias, and was formerly a bonded warehouse.

At the end of the road turn left and carry on to the Cobb, the massive jetty that featured in the posters for "The French Lieutenant's Woman". You can walk along the top of the Cobb (the Upper Walk), or to the left of it (the Lower Walk). The conical fossil casts in the top of the Cobb are called "Portland screws". The alcove in the side wall is called the Gin Shop. There are steps up before it and after it. Farther along is the flight of steps called Granny's Teeth, referred to earlier. This consists of no more than a series of stone slabs jutting out from the wall.

BRIDPORT

Since the thirteenth century Bridport has been the principal town in Britain for the manufacture of ropes and nets. It remains so to this day, and the nets for both Wembley Stadium and the Wimbledon tennis courts were made in the town. Hardy's name for Bridport is Port Bredy.

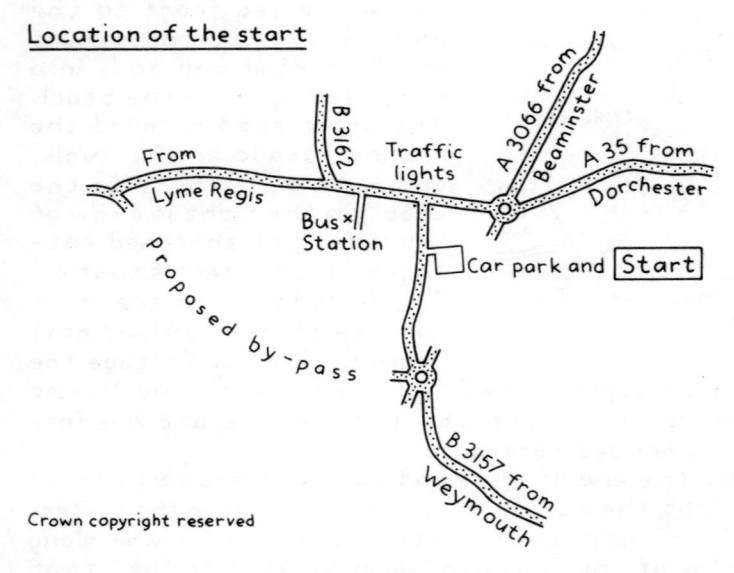

Location of the start

Crown copyright reserved

From the lane running along the side of the car park, turn left into South Street. This was the main street of the Saxon town; and the line of the buildings bulges outwards to accomodate the Saxon market. The market still takes place on Wednesdays and Saturdays, and the position of the stalls is indicated by white lines on the pavement. South of the church, on the left-hand side of

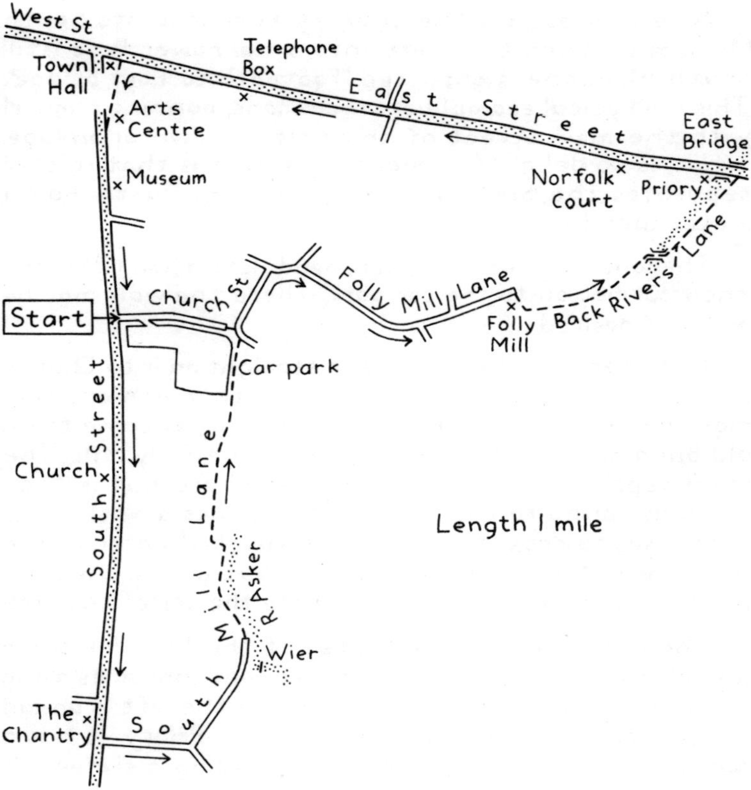
West St
Town Hall
Telephone Box
East Street
East Bridge
Arts Centre
Museum
Norfolk Court
Priory
Lane
Church St
Folly Mill Lane
Back Rivers
Start
Folly Mill
Car park
South Street
Church
Lane
Length 1 mile
South Mill
R. Asker
Wier
The Chantry
South

the road, is an unbroken line of charming eighteenth century cottages, each slightly different from the rest, yet blending together perfectly.

On the right hand side of the road, on the corner of South Walk, is Bridport's oldest house, the Chantry, which is variously described as thirteenth, fourteenth or fifteenth century.

A few yards past the Chantry turn left into South Mill Lane. Then turn left into a narrower lane (still South Mill Lane) signposted "Footpath to East Bridge". This is a typical example of a back lane, running parallel with the main street of an ancient town or village. What is so delightful about this lane is that it still separates the built-up area from the surrounding water meadows.

The lane narrows to a path, bends left, then right, and then carries on to the car park, where the walk may be ended if desired.

At the end of the path, keep straight on into Church Street. Turn right at the T-junction, then immediately right again, and keep on the road until you come to an old building on the right. This was the Folly Mill. The road appears to come to a dead end here, but in fact it bends round to the right and becomes a path. The path rises to cross the leat that supplied water to the mill. The leat has now been filled in, but where the path bends left you can look back and see the top of the arch.

The path follows the course of the leat for some distance, then crosses the River Asker and continues along the river bank to the East Bridge. On the left is an old house which was once part of St John's Priory. It has a number of interesting features including a sixteenth century oriel window.

Turn left at the bridge into East Street, which was the main street of the mediaeval town and has many fine eighteenth and nineteenth century houses. Norfolk Court, on the left, is a good example of a modern building that harmonises with the older buildings without attempting to imitate them.

Many of the alleyways leading off the main streets of

Bridport 15

Bridport were formerly used as ropewalks. One of these is Asker Terrace, which leaves East Street under the name of "C.E. Legg and Co." just past Norfolk Court.

One thing that is pleasing about small towns is that the surrounding countryside can often be seen from the town centre; and as you pass the telephone box you can see the local landmark of Colmer's Hill with its tuft of trees. Sometimes there is an artist here.

The building with the clock tower and cupola is the Town Hall, which stands at the centre of the town. Just before this on the right is a picturesque bow-windowed shop bearing the inscription "King Charles 2nd came here September 23rd 1651".

Immediately before the Town Hall, turn left into a passage called Bucky Doo. On the left is a courtyard. At the far end is the Arts Centre with its giant Ionic pilasters, and either side are houses with smaller Ionic pillars.

The path now becomes the pavement of South Street. The alley on the left, just past the bus stop, and the cobbled lane directly opposite it, are believed to mark the northern limit of the Saxon town. Further along on the left is an attractive sixteenth century building called the Castle, which is now a museum.

The road eventually leads back to the car park.

West Street is the continuation of East Street beyond the Town Hall. On the right, just past the pedestrian crossing, is the Post Office with its elegant Georgian façade. The last building on the right before the road narrows is the rope and net factory. Then the River Brit follows the road and disappears under the West Mill, which is now an architect's office.

BEAMINSTER

Beaminster is a small town, hardly more than a village, but it contains a number of interesting features. It is pronounced Bemminster. Hardy's name for the town is Emminster.

Location of the Start

From the town centre follow the signposts to the car park.

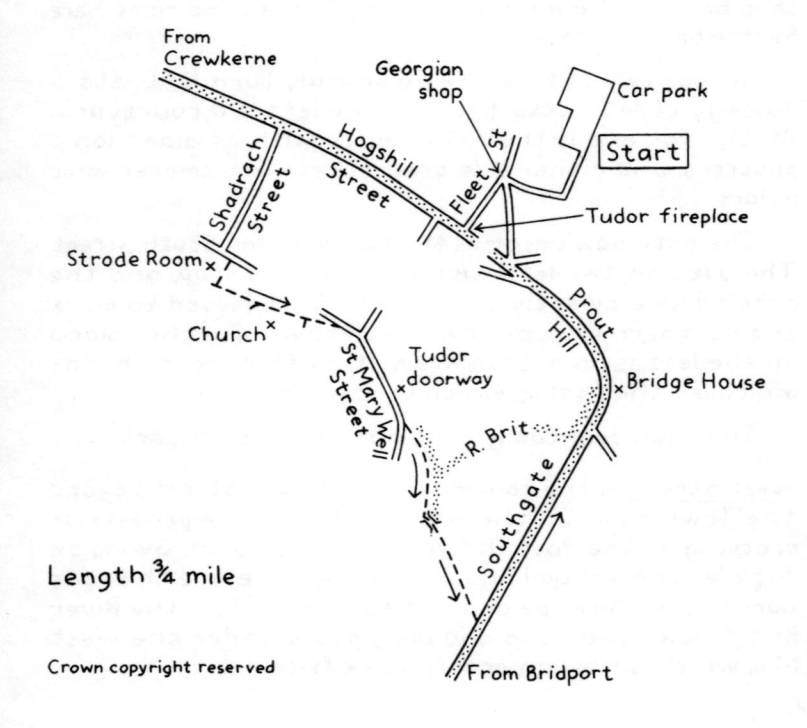

Length ¾ mile

Crown copyright reserved

Beaminster

Opposite the entrance to the car park is a bow-windowed grocery shop which was established in 1780, and which would appear to have been built at about that time. Turn left here (but not sharp left). At the end of the road on the left is an interesting curiosity —a Tudor fireplace that faces outwards into the road. I can't believe that there was ever a room where the road is now.

Turn right here, into the main road. In a hundred yards turn left into Shadrack Street. At the end of the road turn left into Church Street, then immediately right up some steps. The cottage-like building on the right is the Strode Room, which is used for meetings. Turn left through a gate into the churchyard. Here it is worth stopping for a moment to watch the jackdaws flying round the church tower, and to admire the many gargoyles, statues and pinnacles that adorn the tower.

Leave the churchyard by the double gates, and bear right at the Eight Bells into St Mary Well Street. One of the houses on the left (number 5) has a Tudor doorway. At the fork, bear left onto a footpath running along the side of a stream. The stream merges with the River Brit, which is crossed by the path. The weir here was built to supply water to a mill.

Keep on the path to the main road, then turn left. After about a hundred yards the River Brit flows along the left-hand side of the road, and all the houses behind it are approached by bridges. On the right is Bridge House, a very fine seventeenth century house with stone-mullioned windows. At the no entry sign bear right, passing between the Greyhound Hotel and a very old house with an inscription in the gable. At the next junction turn right for the car park.

DORCHESTER

Dorchester is the oldest town in Dorset. It became the tribal capital of the area in A.D. 70, and it remains the County Town. The Roman name for the town is Durnovaria, and Hardy's name for it is Casterbridge.

Location of the start

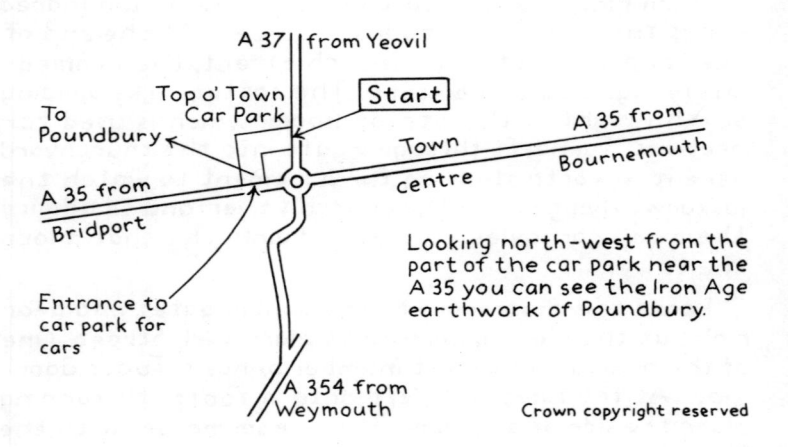

Map showing: A 37 from Yeovil; Top o' Town Car Park; Start; A 35 from Bournemouth; To Poundbury; Town centre; A 35 from Bridport; Entrance to car park for cars; A 354 from Weymouth.

Looking north-west from the part of the car park near the A 35 you can see the Iron Age earthwork of Poundbury.

Crown copyright reserved

Leave the car park by the east entrance. On the opposite side of the road is a bronze life-size statue of Thomas Hardy, who lived in or near Dorchester for most of his life. Hardy is best known for his novels, but he also wrote a great many poems, including the one beginning "This is the weather the cuckoo likes".

Cross over the road, and turn left into a path which runs through an avenue of trees. The name of the path is Colliton Walk, but Hardy called it Chalk Walk. This is

Dorchester

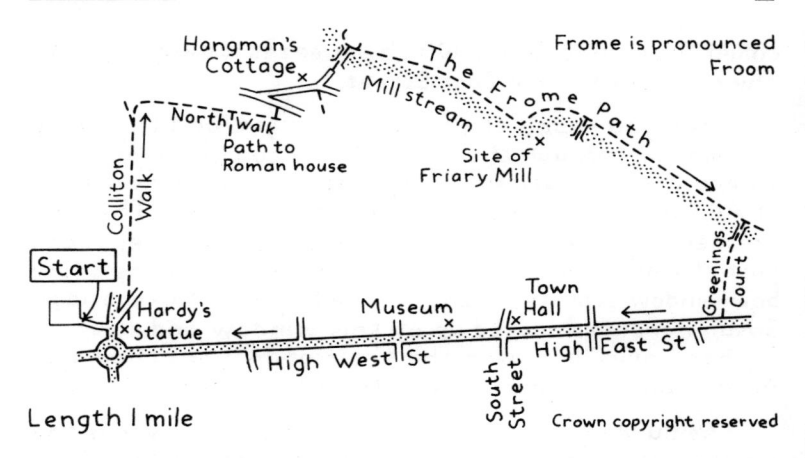

Map showing route: Start at Hardy's Statue, up Colliton Walk, past Path to Roman house, North Walk, Hangman's Cottage, along Mill stream / The Frome Path, past Site of Friary Mill, down Greenings Court, along East St, High East St (Town Hall), High West St (Museum), South Street, back to Start.

Length 1 mile

Frome is pronounced Froom

Crown copyright reserved

where, in "The Mayor of Casterbridge", Henchard tried to persuade Farfrae not to leave the town.

Colliton Walk lies on the line of the west wall of the Roman town, and when it curves round to the right it follows the curved corner of the Roman wall. Some distance past the corner is a gate on the right which leads to the foundations of a Roman house. Just past the gate turn left down a flight of steps, then left into a road, and then immediately sharp right into another road. On the left is the sixteenth century Hangman's Cottage, which also features in Hardy's work.

At the end of the road cross over the mill stream and turn right, following the river bank. Two hundred yards along is the site of the Friary Mill. It is unusual for a water mill to disappear without leaving any trace, and here the evidence is a sudden turn to the left and a narrowing of the course of the stream. The path follows the stream to the left and then to the right. Ignore the first bridge, just past the bends, but cross the second bridge, 200 yards farther on. This leads to the alleyway called Greenings Court, which squeezes its way through the cottages to High East Street.

When you reach the road turn right, and then keep straight on through the town centre to the roundabout where the walk began. The steeple on the left is that of All Saints' Church, which is now redundant. The tiny dormer windows in the spire are called lucarnes. Just past this on the right is the King's Arms, which has a fine bow window over its porch. In "The Mayor of Casterbridge" Susan Henchard looked up at this window and saw her husband presiding over the table as Mayor. The King's Arms is also featured in "Far from the Madding Crowd".

The building on the right with the clock tower is the nineteenth century Town Hall. Next to this is St Peter's Church, which is fifteenth century. Outside it is a bronze statue of William Barnes, Dorset's second most famous poet. His best-known poem is "Linden Lea".

Next comes the Dorset County Museum with its intricately carved windows, and then, on the other side of the road, is Judge Jeffreys' Lodging, a beautiful seventeenth century half-timbered building, now a restaurant. On the first floor is a little door that leads out onto a balcony.

Near the top of the hill on the right is the Old Tea House, which was built in 1635. The fireplace was recently opened up revealing a solid bressumer. A twelfth century manuscript was found in the chimney, and this is now displayed inside the tea room.

Longer alternative

Instead of crossing over the mill stream into Greenings Court, continue along the stream to the main road. Cross over the road and take the turning opposite. After a

Dorchester

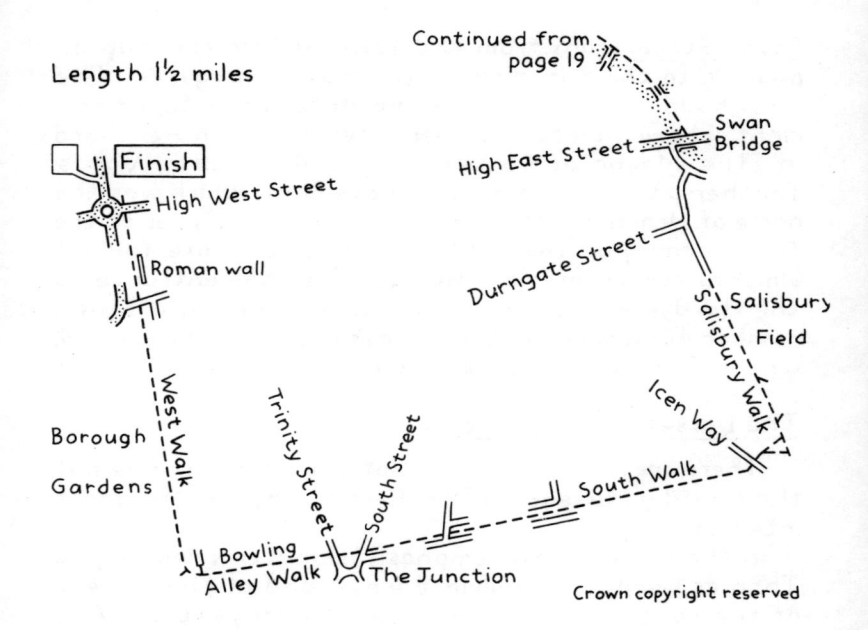

Length 1½ miles

few yards bear slightly right, and at the next junction slightly left. At the end of the road carry straight on through an avenue of horse chestnut trees that follows the course of the Roman wall round three sides of the town, as shown on the map.

Salisbury Walk runs along the side of the open space called Salisbury Field. Bowling Alley Walk follows a grassy strip out of sight of any traffic; and West Walk runs along the side of a park. All in all the Walks provide a peaceful alternative to the route back through the town centre. Alongside the very last stretch of the Walks is the only surviving section of the Roman town wall.

Dorchester

<u>South Street</u> runs from the Town Hall (on the map on page 19) to the Junction (on the map on page 21). The first building of interest is the Antelope Hotel on the right, where Lucetta had her interview with Henchard in "The Mayor of Casterbridge". A hundred yards farther on on the left is Barclay's Bank, which was the home of Henchard, as indicated by a plaque. Opposite the first turning on the right is the Napper's Mite, former almshouses built in 1616. Then, opposite the entrance to the Hardye Arcade, are two houses bearing plaques, number 40, where William Barnes lived, and number 39, where Thomas Hardy worked in an architect's office.

The Dorset County Museum

There are museums in most of the Dorset towns, but the County Museum in Dorchester is by far the most interesting.

In the main hall the emphasis is on items relating to Thomas Hardy and William Barnes; and at the far end of the room is a reconstruction of Hardy's study. Also on the ground floor is an exhibition of paintings which are regularly changed, and an excellent collection of old farm equipment.

Upstairs there is so much to see that several visits are needed to do justice to it. In the Geological Gallery there are displays explaining the structure of various places of scenic interest, and there is a colourful geological model of the county.

In the Natural History Gallery there are sections on the flowers of Portland, houses and gardens, the sea, flowers of shingle beaches, heathland, freshwater, woodland, conifer plantations, insects, grassland and the classification of plants and animals.

Finally, in the Archaeological Gallery there are displays relating to each of the prehistoric periods.

WEYMOUTH

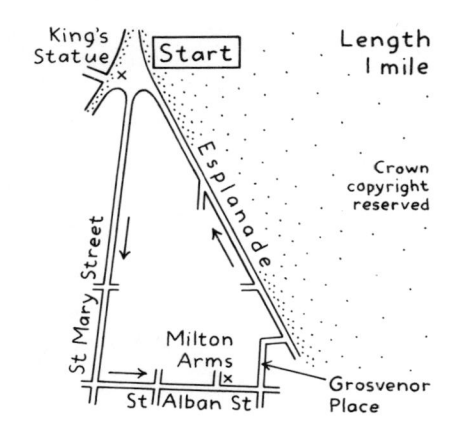

Length 1 mile

Crown copyright reserved

Strictly speaking, this walk is in Melcombe Regis, and Weymouth is on the other side of the River Wey, but in practice the whole town is referred to as Weymouth. Hardy's name for the town is Budmouth.

Weymouth is the terminal for the ferries to Cherbourg and the Channel Islands.

The trail starts at the statue of King George III on the sea front. Behind the statue are two great curving Georgian façades. Pass between them into St Mary Street. At the second crossroads turn left into St Alban Street, a narrow lane of great charm. On the left is the Milton Arms, which has an Elizabethan doorway.

At the next crossroads turn left into Grosvenor Place, whose pink-washed holiday flats are just right for a seaside resort. Cross over the Esplanade and turn left. On the right is a beautiful view across Weymouth Bay to St Aldhelm's Head. The Esplanade leads back to the statue.

Extension

Follow the Esplanade to the north from the statue. On the left is the Gloucester Hotel, which, apart from the first six bays, was the summer residence of King

24   Weymouth

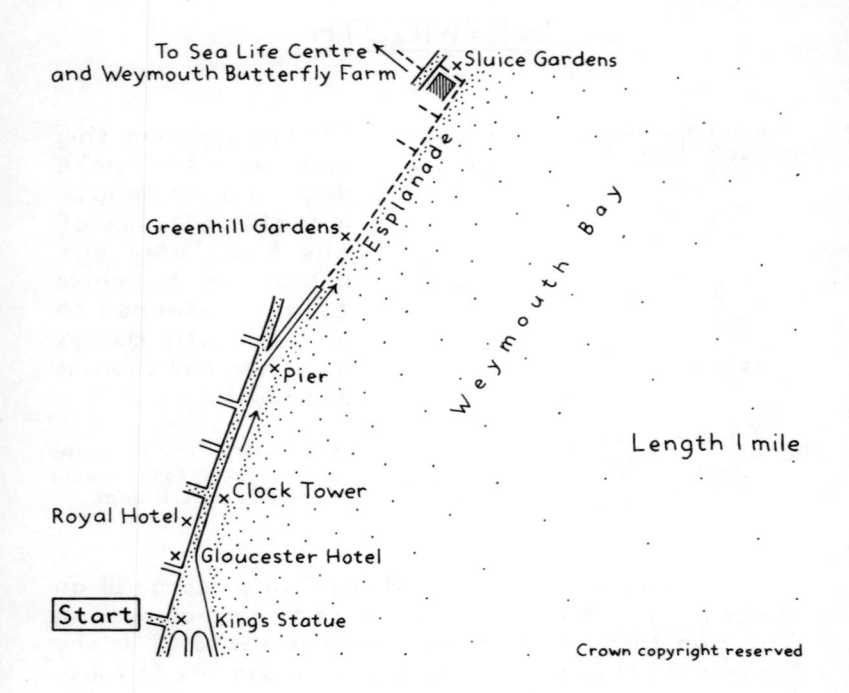

Map showing Weymouth seafront walk from Start at King's Statue, past Gloucester Hotel, Royal Hotel, Clock Tower, Pier, Greenhill Gardens, along the Esplanade to Sluice Gardens, with route To Sea Life Centre and Weymouth Butterfly Farm. Weymouth Bay to the right. Length 1 mile.

Crown copyright reserved

George III from 1789 until 1805. The beginning of Weymouth as a seaside resort dates from this period.

Farther along on the left is the Royal Hotel, a splendid example of late Victorian architecture. At the Clock Tower, the character of the beach changes, and the sand gives way to shingle.

When you reach the pier, continue along the esplanade, passing Greenhill Gardens with its floral clock. The Osmington White Horse is now visible straight ahead. At the end of the built-up area turn left, then left into the main road, and then immediately right along a path. On the right is the Model World, and beyond

Weymouth

it the Sea Life Centre, the Butterfly Farm and other places of interest.

<u>The Model World</u> consists of a succession of models set out in a garden and linked by a path. There are three villages, a town, two castles, two mansions, a cathedral, a ruined abbey, two farms, a railway, a water-mill, a windmill, a circus, a zoo, a fairground, an airport and a space centre, all built to the same scale and all constructed by one man. Many of the models have amusing names such as "Hugh Sinkham's Boat Yard".

<u>The Weymouth Butterfly Farm</u> was opened by David Bellamy in 1984, and is open from March 15th until October 30th. The entrance is approached through the Wild Flower Meadow. The flowers planted here can be found anywhere in the countryside, but not in such profusion.

From the meadow you pass into the shop, and from there you push your way through a screen of overlapping plastic sheets into the Main Flight Area. However cold it is outside, the temperature in here is always 75°F. There are butterflies from all over the world, and because they are flying all round you, you feel as though you are actually observing them in the wild. There are also caterpillars here, feeding on the plants, though you don't notice them at first. The chrysalises are kept together in the Butterfly Hatching Cages to give visitors the chance to watch the butterflies emerging and stretching their wings.

From the Main Flight Area you pass through another plastic screen into the Caterpillar and Insect Breeding House. Here you can watch a forty-minute video film about the London Butterfly House, and see red-legged tarantulas, stick insects, giant atlas moths and other insects. You can also watch leaf-cutting ants carrying pieces of leaf along a glass tube to their nest.

SHERBORNE

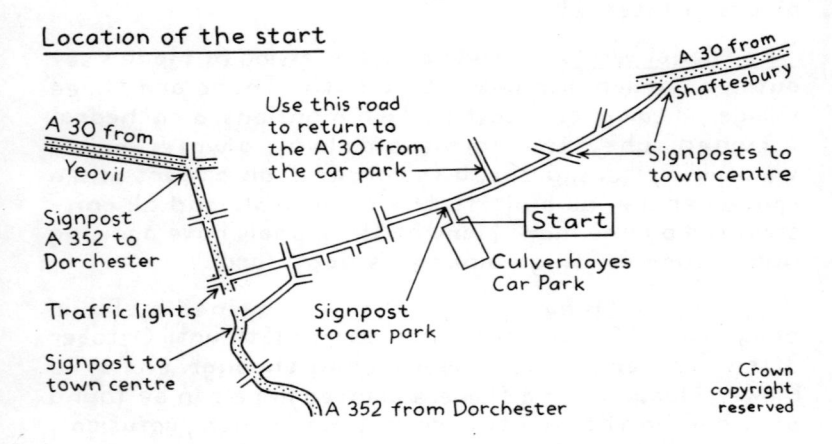

Location of the start

(Map showing location of the start at Culverhayes Car Park, with labels: A 30 from Shaftesbury, A 30 from Yeovil, Signpost A 352 to Dorchester, Traffic lights, Signpost to town centre, A 352 from Dorchester, Use this road to return to the A 30 from the car park, Signposts to town centre, Signpost to car park, Start, Culverhayes Car Park.)

Crown copyright reserved

From Culverhayes Car Park turn left into Long Street. This is the road that links the Old Castle with the Abbey, and it contains a number of interesting buildings. On the left is Abbots Litton, a very attractive Georgian house with a fine porch. Next to it is the Old Bank House, which was built in the sixteenth century.

The hexagonal building facing you at the end of the street is the sixteenth century Conduit House. In the centre of the ceiling is the Shield of Arms of Sherborne Abbey, incorporating a crozier, or staff carried by a bishop or abbot.

From here onwards it is necessary to walk slowly, stopping frequently, because there is so much to see. The Conduit House stands in an open space called the Parade, which was formerly called the Shambles. Pass to the left of the Conduit House, and keep straight on into Church Lane. This was formerly called Underbow because it passes through the fifteenth century archway

Sherborne   27

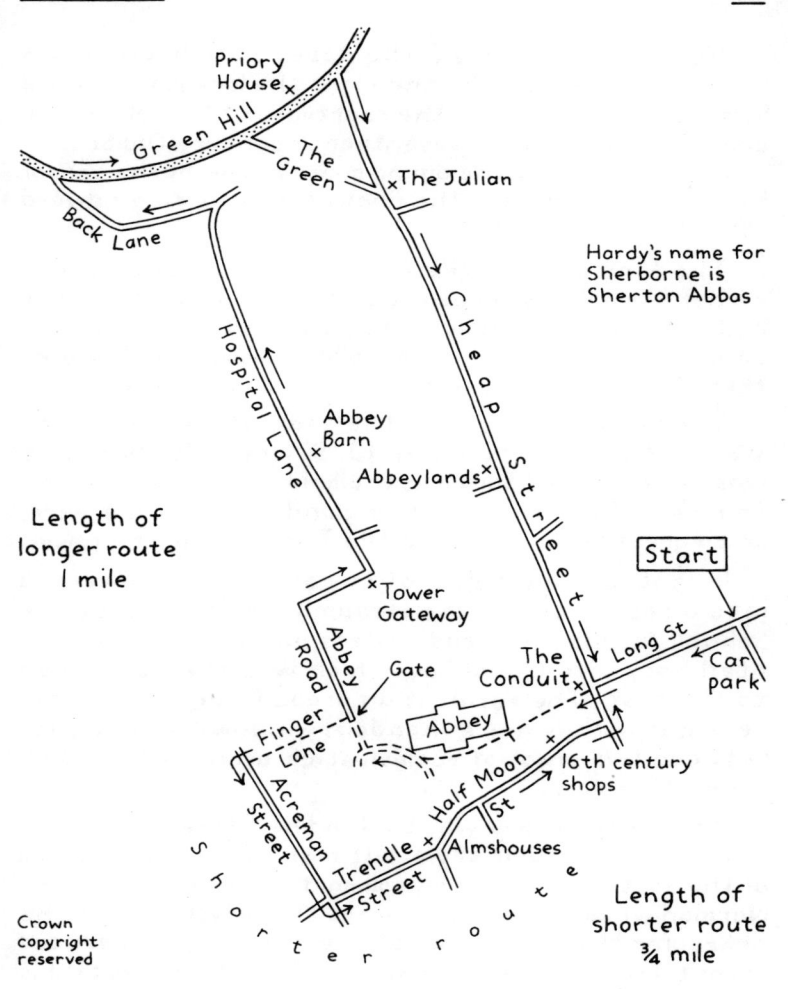

Map labels:
- Priory House
- Green Hill
- The Green
- The Julian
- Back Lane
- Cheap Street
- Hospital Lane
- Abbey Barn
- Abbeylands
- Start
- Long St
- Car park
- Tower Gateway
- Abbey Road
- Gate
- The Conduit
- Finger Lane
- Abbey
- Acreman Street
- Half Moon St
- 16th century shops
- Trendle Street
- Almshouses
- Shorter route

Hardy's name for Sherborne is Sherton Abbas

Length of longer route 1 mile

Length of shorter route ¾ mile

Crown copyright reserved

called the Cemetery Gate or the Bow. Above the archway are two niches with carved stonework.

Beyond the archway is the Abbey Gate House, which houses the museum. On the right the lane is separated by a high stone wall from the courtyard of School Barton, and behind that is the seventeenth century Old Schoolhouse, which is now the dining room of Sherborne School. Between its windows is the Coat of Arms of King Edward VI.

The lane leads to the Abbey Close, an open space rather like a village green, with the Abbey on the right and old stone cottages at the far end. This is where Giles Winterborne and Grace Melbury walked and planned their future in Hardy's novel "The Woodlanders".

Sherborne Abbey was the seat of the Bishop of Wessex from A.D. 705 until 1075, when the bishopric was moved to Old Sarum. Ethelbald and Ethelbert, the third and fourth kings of England, were buried here, and a great tenor bell called Old Tom hangs in the tower.

In 1560 the east end of the abbey was converted into a residence for the Headmaster of Sherborne School. In 1919 the headmaster's house was incorporated back into the abbey, which was then extended to the east. The result is an area of domestic architecture with square-headed windows sandwiched between two areas of ecclesiastical architecture with pointed windows.

Most of the abbey was built in the fifteenth century in the Perpendicular style, but high up on the east wall of the South Transept is a small part of a twelfth century Norman window. Even this is not the oldest part of the abbey, for the rubble wall of the west end (illustrated opposite) is tenth century Saxon. At right angles to this wall is the end gable of the Guest Hall, which is now the school library. The walls and buttresses are thirteenth century, but the windows were added later.

Sherborne 29

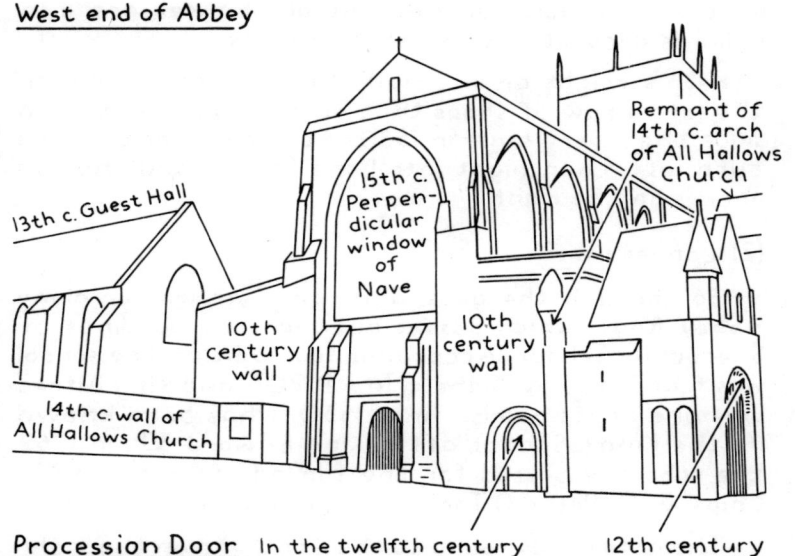

West end of Abbey

Labels on illustration:
- 13th c. Guest Hall
- 15th c. Perpendicular window of Nave
- Remnant of 14th c. arch of All Hallows Church
- 10th century wall
- 10th century wall
- 14th c. wall of All Hallows Church
- 12th century archway with chevron moulding

<u>Procession Door</u> In the twelfth century a doorway was built into the tenth century wall. Then it was blocked up. In the fourteenth century it was opened up again, then it was blocked up again. As a result there is a wall in an arch in a wall in an arch in a wall to fascinate students of mediaeval architecture.

(1) Shorter route

Go through the gate and immediately turn left into an alley called Finger Lane. At the end of the alley turn left into Acreman Street. Then turn left again into Trendle Street. At the far end of this street on the left is St John's Almshouses, a remarkably well preserved fifteenth century building, with the original door and windows all intact. Either side of the doorway are carved niches similar to those over the Cemetery Gate but in better condition. Outside the almshouses are iron bollards decorated with bishops' mitres.

Keep straight on into Half Moon Street, passing on the left a row of shops that have hardly been altered since they were built in 1530. At the end of the road turn left, then right into Long Street, and the car park is on the right.

(2) Longer route

Go through the gate, and carry straight on along Abbey Road, which passes between the buildings of Sherborne School. According to tradition, the school was founded by St Aldhelm in A.D. 705, and King Alfred was one of its pupils. Since 1550 it has been known as the King's School, after King Edward VI. In 1969 the school was used for the filming of "Goodbye Mr Chips" with Peter O'Toole and Petula Clark.

The road bends round to the right, and on the right is the Tower Gateway, with the coat of arms of Edward VI over the entrance. Follow the road round to the left, and go straight on at the next junction.

On the right is the present Headmaster's house, which was converted from the fifteenth century Abbey Barn in 1827. The original entrance to the barn can be seen below the south-facing gable. The window above it is also original. To the right of the second-floor window in the west-facing gable is the shield of arms of Sherborne Abbey.

Beyond this house, on the left, is a stretch of old flagstone pavement. The trees overhanging the road farther up are holm oaks. When the road bends right, turn left into Back Lane. Follow this round to the right, and turn sharp right into Green Hill.

Sherborne 31

Green Hill is part of the A 30, which runs from London to Land's End. The pavements are set ten feet or so above the roadway. Either side are old stone cottages with names such as Monks Newell, Tuffins Passage and September Cottage.

The first turning on the right is the Green, which was the site of the Gooseberry Fair from 1240 until 1888. In the angle between Green Hill and the Green the inscription "licenced to let post horses" can be made out over the porch of a house.

Continue along the main road. On the left is a battlemented house with diamond-leaded windows. This is where Horace Vachell the author spent his last years.

Turn right opposite the Antelope Hotel into Higher Cheap Street. Just past the George Hotel on the left is the Julian, a sixteenth century building with a two-storey bay added in the seventeenth century. Keep straight on into Cheap Street, which was the main street of the town in Saxon times and remains so today. Hardy called it Sheep Street.

Some way down on the right, on the corner of Abbey Road, is the house called Abbeylands, now a dormitory for Sherborne School. Over the door is the date 1649, but this refers to the stone part of the house. The half-timbered part is Elizabethan. The first floor oriel window on the right is obviously a modern reconstruction, but we can tell that the rest of the building is original by the carpenters' marks. These are the Roman numbers carved on the horizontal beam halfway up the first floor and on some of the vertical beams.

Before long you will recognise the hexagonal Conduit House on the right. Turn left here, and the car park is on the right.

SHAFTESBURY

Like Bridport, Shaftesbury has a Saxon town and a mediaeval town. The Saxon town is situated on a ridge 700 feet above sea level, with glorious views to north and south. Many of the older houses are built of greensand. Hardy's name for Shaftesbury is Shaston.

Location of the start

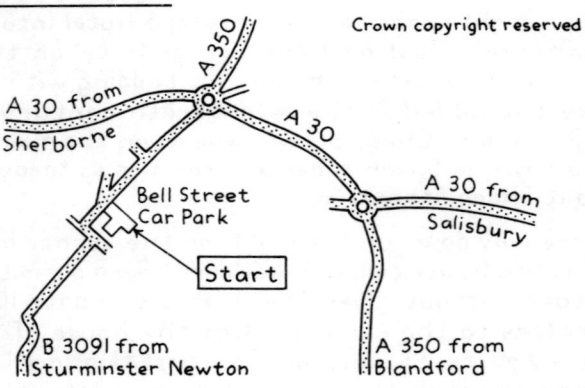

Crown copyright reserved

Leave the car park by the south-east entrance. Turn right into Bell Street, and left at the Commons into High Street. Where High Street bends left the battlemented Town Hall is seen on the right. At the far end of the Town Hall turn right into a narrow cobbled lane with the ancient stonework of St Peter's church on the left.

Shaftesbury 33

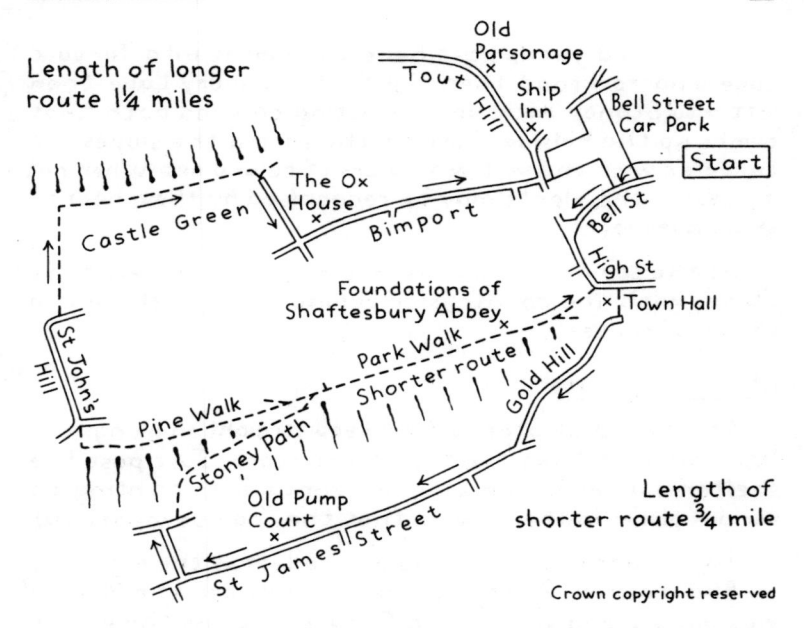

Map showing routes around Shaftesbury, including Old Parsonage, Tout Hill, Ship Inn, Bell Street Car Park, Start, Bell St, The Ox House, Bimport, Castle Green, High St, Town Hall, Foundations of Shaftesbury Abbey, Park Walk, Shorter route, Gold Hill, St John's Hill, Pine Walk, Stoney Path, Old Pump Court, St James Street. Length of longer route 1¼ miles. Length of shorter route ¾ mile.

Crown copyright reserved

The lane comes out into Gold Hill. On the right is the Abbey Wall with its mighty mediaeval buttresses. On the left is a group of charming cottages arranged down the hillside in steps. Underfoot are cobblestones, and in the distance is the beautiful Dorset countryside. These four things have combined to make Gold Hill the most photographed street in Dorset, and the setting for innumerable scenes in films and on television.

At the foot of Gold Hill bear right into St James's Street, which leads to the mediaeval suburb of St James. This is consistently attractive, with grey stone houses along both sides of the road. Especially pleasing is Old Pump Court on the right, where the buildings are ranged round three sides of a courtyard with a pump in the centre.

A hundred yards past here turn right into Tanyard Lane, a narrow road, then right into Laundry Lane, then left into Stoney Path, an interesting cobbled path that climbs up the hillside. Early in the spring the slopes are carpeted with the yellow flowers of celandines. When not in flower the plants may be recognised by their heart-shaped leaves.

At the top of the hill there is an excellent view of St James with the countryside behind it. Here there is a choice of routes.

(1) Shorter route

At the top of Stoney Path keep straight on along Park Walk, which follows the top of the scarp. Just past the shelter is an indicator with horizontal lines pointing to various places in the view, so that they can be identified.

Two hundred yards along on the left is the entrance to Shaftesbury Abbey, where King Edward the Martyr was buried, and where King Canute died. At the end of Park Walk, bear left along a path to the town centre. Turn left into High Street, and so back to the car park.

(2) Longer route

At the top of Stoney Path turn sharp left into Pine Walk, a metalled path which runs through the trees along the side of the hill. The path goes round a right-hand bend and comes out into a road. Keep straight on along the road, and just a few yards past a sharp right-hand bend turn left through a little green gate onto a metalled path.

This follows the left-hand side of Castle Green, and after it bends right it runs along the top of the northern scarp. There is an indicator here, just as there is on the

Shaftesbury 35

southern scarp. Among the places identified are Glastonbury Tor, the Quantocks and Alfred's Tower.

Glastonbury Tor   Alfred's Tower

At the end of the green turn right. Carry on until you come to a road, and turn left. This is Bimport, the main street of the Saxon town, but it lacks the charm of Bridport's Saxon street. The third house on the left has stone-mullioned windows that have been converted into sash windows. It was built early in the seventeenth century and is called the Ox House. Hardy called it Old Grove's Place and made it the home of Richard and Sue Phillotson in "Jude the Obscure".

Continue on the road to the T-junction, where the car park will be seen straight ahead.

Tout Hill is like a mirror image of Gold Hill, for just as Gold Hill curves round the south-east corner of the Abbey Precinct, so Tout Hill curves round the northeast corner, and in both cases the precinct is bounded by a high mediaeval wall. From the ancient Ship Inn a very attractive high pavement follows the road down to the Old Parsonage, where road and pavement are linked by old stone steps.

Shaftesbury Avenue in London was named not after the town, but after the Earl of Shaftesbury, who lived twelve miles away at Wimborne St Giles.

STURMINSTER NEWTON

Dorset's longest river, the Stour, flows through three towns with double-barrelled names. These are Sturminster Newton, Blandford Forum and Wimborne Minster. The names of the last two are usually shortened to Blandford and Wimborne, but the name of Sturminster Newton is usually given in full. Hardy's name for the town is Stourcastle.

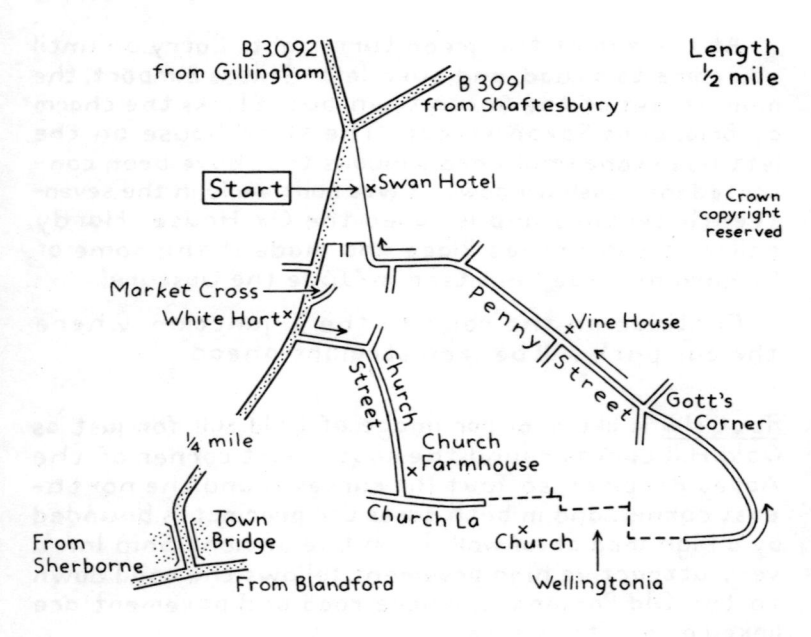

Length ½ mile

Crown copyright reserved

The trail starts outside the Swan Hotel in the Market Place. The street is wedge-shaped, narrow at the north end, and wide enough at the south end to continue as three roads with buildings in between them.

Sturminster Newton 37

Take the right-hand road. On the left is the fifteenth century Market Cross where William Barnes used to sit on the steps. On the right is the White Hart, an old-fashioned public house bearing the date 1708. Just past this turn left, and then turn right into an attractive lane. The last house on the left, Church Farmhouse, is built of the local cream-coloured stone called Coral Rag. Turn left at the junction, and at the end of the road carry straight on along the left-hand side of the churchyard.

The path bends right, then left. In the churchyard is an excellent specimen of a Wellingtonia or Big Tree. This tree is sometimes confused with the redwood, but it may be distinguished by its twigs, which are covered in pointed scales.

At the T-junction turn right. The path goes round a left-hand bend and becomes a road. Follow the road round to the left and over the little cross-roads called Gott's Corner. Opposite the next turning on the left is a beautiful seventeenth-century house called Vine House. This is where William Barnes worked in a solicitor's office before he became known as a poet.

After the road bends slightly left, notice how the upper stories of the cottages on the left overhang the ground floor. This is called jettying, and indicates that hidden behind the plaster are some very old timber-framed houses.

After the next junction the road bends round to the right and leads back to the Market Square.

There are disused water mills all along the Dorset rivers, but at Sturminster Newton there is one that is still working. It is situated on the Sherborne road 200 yards west of the Town Bridge, and is open to the public on Tuesdays, Thursdays, Saturdays and Sundays from May to September.

BLANDFORD FORUM

Map showing one-way streets and the location of the start

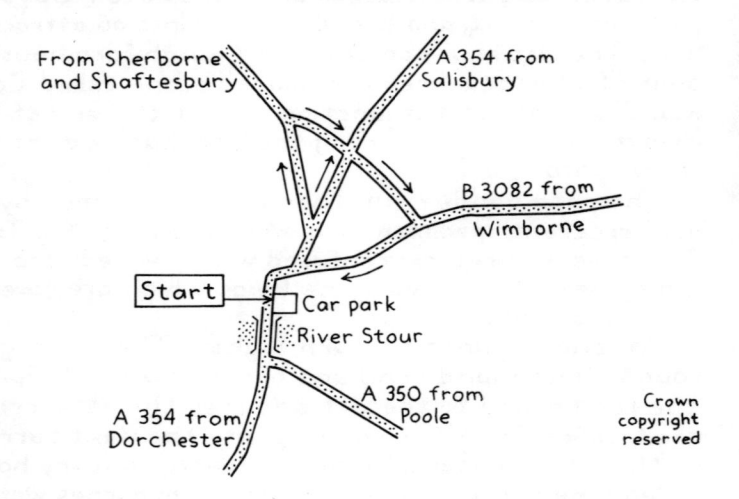

From Sherborne and Shaftesbury
A 354 from Salisbury
B 3082 from Wimborne
Start — Car park
River Stour
A 354 from Dorchester
A 350 from Poole

Crown copyright reserved

Turn right out of the car park into West Street, which is lined by Georgian houses in the style for which Blandford is noted. At the Market Place bear left into Salisbury Street. Just past the fork turn right into a street with the interesting name of The Plocks. This opens out into a little square where sheep used to be kept before being taken to the market. Lyme Tree House on the right is a good example of a Blandford-style house with red bricks round the windows and vitrified bricks beyond.

From the opposite side of the square a road leads to another open space called the Tabernacle, where the sheep market used to be held. In the middle of the space is an oak tree which was planted in 1905.

Blandford Forum   39

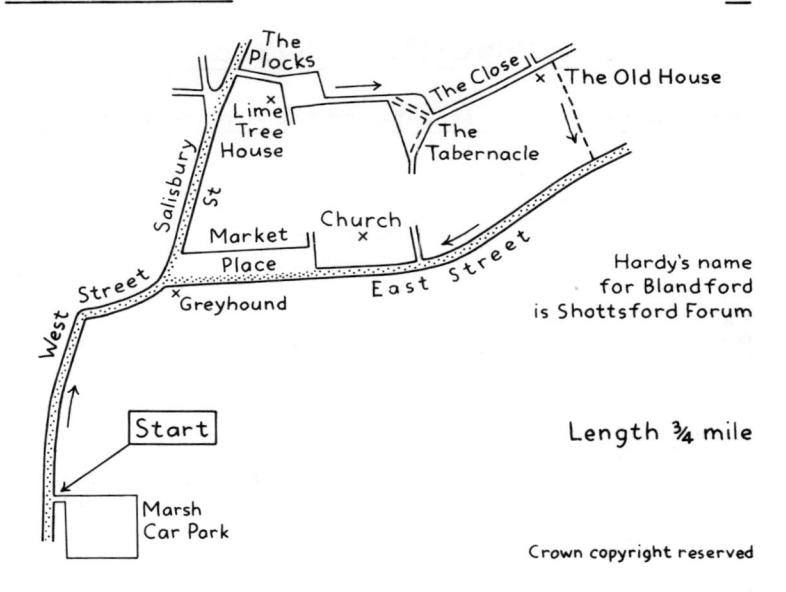

[Map showing route through Blandford Forum with labels: The Plocks, Lime Tree House, Salisbury St, The Close, The Old House, The Tabernacle, Market Place, Church, East Street, Greyhound, West Street, Start, Marsh Car Park]

Hardy's name for Blandford is Shottsford Forum

Length ¾ mile

Crown copyright reserved

Carry straight on into the Close. Opposite the first turning on the left is the Old House, which is remarkable for its ornamental brickwork. Note particularly the chimneys and the panel over the door.

Just beyond the Old House turn right into a passage. At the bottom of the Hill turn right into East Street, which leads back to the Market Place. On the right is the church, which is built of greensand. Just past it is the Fire Memorial, which was erected in 1760 to commemorate the fire of 1731.

On both sides of the Market Place are fine Georgian buildings. Halfway along on the right is the stone Town Hall, and at the far end on the left is the Greyhound, whose top two stories are particularly impressive.

At the end of the Market Place bear left into West Street, which leads back to the car park.

WIMBORNE MINSTER

Map showing one-way streets and the location of the start

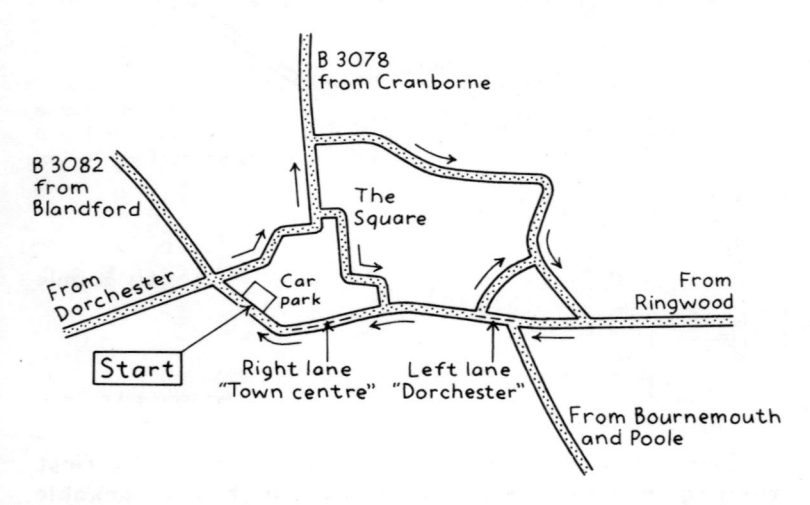

Leave the main part of the car park by a road with a horse chestnut tree in the middle of it. Pass through the extension to the car park, and leave it by a sign marked "Exit".

Turn right in the churchyard, across the front of the great West Tower of Wimborne Minster. Close to the tower is a sundial mounted on a pillar and bearing the date 1676. Turn left here, and then right at the south porch, which is no longer used.

On either side of the path are rose bushes with sweet-scented flowers of various colours. Behind you is the south side of the Minster, which is similar to the north side, but has the advantage of facing the sun. The main part of the church is built of carstone, a

Wimborne Minster 41

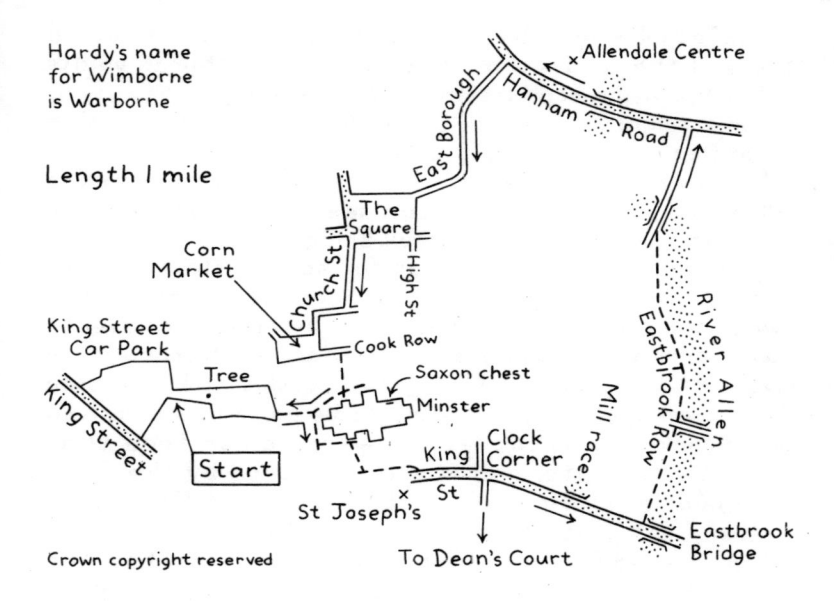

Hardy's name for Wimborne is Warborne

Length 1 mile

[Map showing: Allendale Centre, East Borough, Hanham Road, The Square, Corn Market, Church St, High St, King Street Car Park, Tree, Cook Row, Saxon chest, Minster, King St, Clock Corner, St Joseph's, To Dean's Court, Mill race, Eastbrook Row, River Allen, Eastbrook Bridge, King Street, Start]

Crown copyright reserved

reminder that the heath is not far away. Notice how many different shades of brown there are, particularly between the windows of the clerestory. The West Tower, on the other hand, is built of greensand.

At the end of the path turn left through an avenue of lime trees. The Norman Tower of the Minster is visible on the left, and on the right, across the road, is the half-timbered sixteenth century house called St. Joseph's. The path becomes the pavement of King Street, which leads to the road junction called Clock Corner.

(The narrow road to the right from here leads to the mansion of Dean's Court, whose grounds are open to the public from 2 p.m. to 6 p.m. on Thursdays, Sundays and Bank Holidays in the summer. In the grounds is a vegetable sanctuary, the first in the country, where rare varieties of vegetables may be seen; and there are conducted tours of the cellars that were used as the church vaults in the television production of "Moonfleet".)

Go straight on at Clock Corner (or turn right if coming from Dean's Court), cross over the mill race, and turn left into Eastbrook Row. The river on the right is the Allen, and looking back you can see it flowing under the old stone arches of Eastbrook Bridge.

The path follows the river for some distance. Shoals of tiny fishes can be seen in the clean clear water, while swans and cygnets glide gracefully by. The path eventually becomes the pavement of a road, which crosses the river. At the junction turn left. Outside the Allendale Centre on the right is a remarkable piece of varnished woodwork. It was cut from a weeping ash tree that grew on this site, and it was restored by the Tree Preservation Officer of Wimborne District Council.

Turn left into East Borough, which was formerly called Crooked Borough for obvious reasons. Note how the bricks of the modern building on the right match those of the older buildings farther along on the left. In fact, the modern bricks, with their rough texture and variety of colour, actually look better than the old bricks.

The road comes out into the Square. On the left is a view down the High Street. The old stone building half-way down on the left is the sixteenth century Priest's House, which is now a museum.

Cross over to the far corner of the Square and enter Church Street. At the T-junction turn right into a road that goes round a left-hand bend and comes out into the Cornmarket. This was a focal point of the mediaeval town, and is now a quiet backwater. Turn left here into Cook Row, and then right along a path which leads across Minster Green to the north porch of the Minster.

Wimborne Minster is recognisable in photographs by

Wimborne Minster

its two towers, which are similar in size but quite different in character. The Central Tower is Norman (apart from the parapet), and the West Tower, or Bell Tower, is Perpendicular. In a window of the Bell Tower is the famous Quarter Jack, a life-sized model soldier who strikes his bells every quarter of an hour.

Inside the Bell Tower is the Orrery Clock, an astronomical clock made in 1320 and one of the oldest in the world. In A.D. 871 King Ethelred I, the elder brother of Alfred the Great, was buried in the Minster. Nothing remains of his grave, but there is an oak chest dating from about his time. It is at the east end of the church, close to the north wall, and consists of a large block of wood with a tiny cavity in it.

To get back to the car park turn right at the porch (or left from inside the church), and then bear right.

Wimborne Minster is the subject of Hardy's poem "Copying Architecture in an Old Minster", but I prefer this poem by Will o' Wimborne, which is included here by kind permission of the Editor of the Dorset Year Book. It's called "The Orrery Clock".

> Since Peter Lightfoot journeyed down
>   From Glastonbury to Wimborne Town
> Six hundred years have been and gone,
>   But the clock he fashioned goes ticking on.
> Though kingdoms shake and empires rock,
>   Tick-tock, tick-tock goes the Orrery Clock.
>
> He fashioned it large and strong and square,
>   With wheels and pinions fine and rare,
> And when 'twas well and truly wound
>   The sun and moon began their round.
> "It works, it works, by my cowl and frock!"
>   Tick-tock, tick-tock, said the Orrery Clock.

The poem goes on for a further nine verses, each one ending in a similar way.

WAREHAM

Wareham occupies an interesting position on a strip of land between two parallel rivers, the Piddle and the Frome. It is surrounded on three sides by earth banks called the Town Walls. The circuit of the walls is described in "A Guide to the Isle of Purbeck", and the route described here explores the area within the walls. Hardy's name for Wareham is Anglebury.

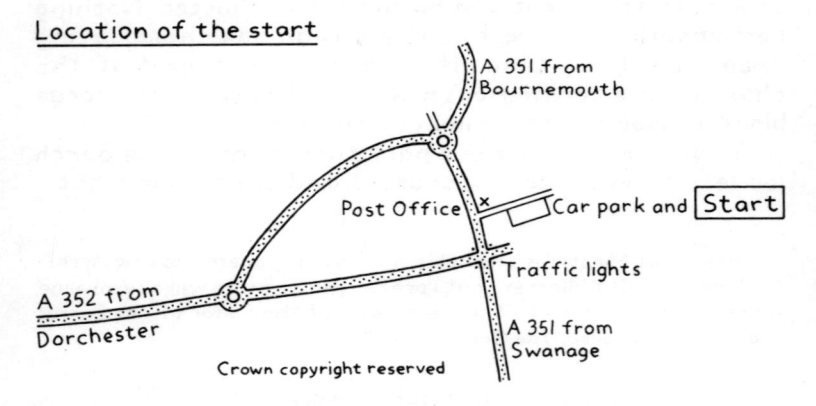

Location of the start

Crown copyright reserved

Turn right out of the car park (away from the Post Office). Turn right into Moreton's Lane, right into East Street and immediately left into Church Street. Ignore the turning into the car park and turn right into St Johns Hill. In the wall on the right you can make out the windows of former cottages.

Farther along on the right is the shop of W.M. Ponds. This was originally a barn that was built in about 1500, and it retains a doorway from this period. There are usually some wattle hurdles outside. For thousands of years hurdles like these have been used for sheepfolds

Wareham

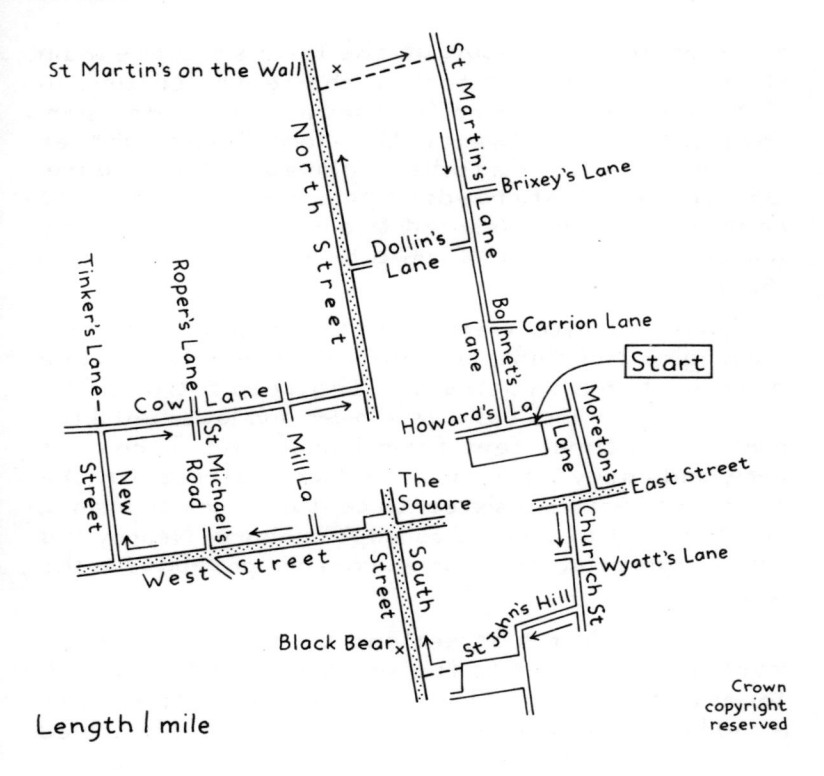

Length 1 mile

and for the walls of timber-framed houses.

Here the road bends left and opens out into a very attractive square. Turn right, and continue along a passage to South Street. The Purbeck Hills are visible in the distance on the left. Cross over the road and turn right, passing through a porch with a figure of a black bear over it, and carry on to the traffic lights.

This crossroads, which is locally known as the Square,

has been the focal point of the town since the main streets were laid out early in the tenth century. In 1958, when I was working for the Forestry Commission, I helped to carry a twenty-five-foot Christmas tree through the forest to be displayed in the Square. On December 31st crowds of people gathered here to celebrate the New Year. At two minutes to midnight we all linked arms to form a huge circle and sang "Auld Lang Syne".

Turn left into West Street, and take the third turning on the right, just before number 42. At the next junction is an attractive thatched cottage. The wall facing Tinker's Lane gets lower and lower until the roof is only three feet from the ground. Turn right here, and carry straight on to North Street. On the right is an enormous sixteenth century chimney breast, which is part of a house called Anglebury. Nearby is a notice saying that traction engines are prohibited in the lane.

Cross over North Street and turn left. The pavement leads straight to the sixteenth century south tower of St Martin's Church. The roof of the tower is saddlebacked, which means simply that it is gabled like the roof of a house.

At the entrance to the church turn right. The eastern part of the church is Saxon, apart from the windows. A very pleasant path leads away from the church through an avenue of trees. The first and third trees on the right are ashes. The last tree on the right is a sweet chestnut. All the rest are oaks.

Turn right into St Martin's Lane. Just past Brixey's Lane is an area of waste ground which is covered in wild flowers. The car park is now straight ahead.

SWANAGE

The four-wheeled pedal cycles seen in Swanage in the summer time are called quikes.

Hardy's name for Swanage is Knollsea.

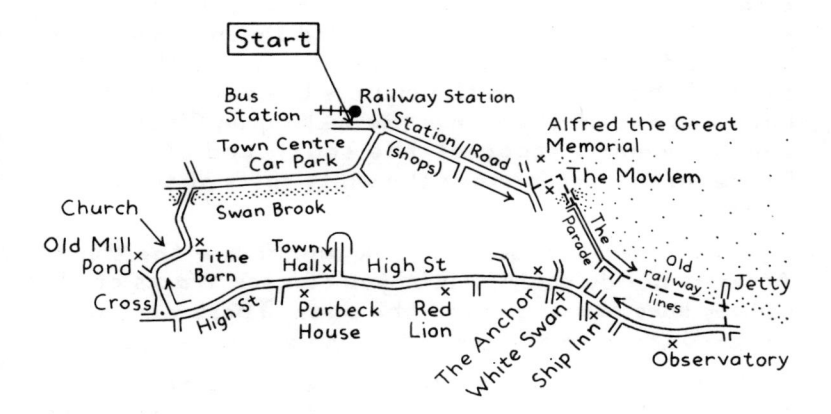

Length 1 mile   Crown copyright reserved

The trail starts at the terminus of the Swanage Steam Railway by the bus station. There is a car park here, but parking is limited to one hour. At present the trains only run as far as Helston Halt a mile away, but it is hoped that they will eventually run to Wareham.

Go straight on at the mini-roundabout into the main shopping street. When this bends right head for the sea, passing along the left-hand side of the Mowlem Theatre. On the left is a sandy beach where children build sand castles in the summer. Nearby is a stone pillar surmounted by four cannon balls. It was erected in 1862 to commemorate a battle fought by King Alfred in Swanage Bay in 877.

At the beach the path bends right and passes under the Mowlem Restaurant. From this restaurant there is a beautiful view, but the view from underneath it is just as good. On the left is Ballard Down, where the brown cliffs of the Wealden beds give way to the white cliffs of the chalk. On the right is the pier, and at the landward end of the pier is the Wellington Clock Tower, which formerly stood at the south end of London Bridge. In the distance are the white cliffs of the Isle of Wight.

Cross over the Swan Brook and follow the shore. After it bends slightly left you can see traces of old railway lines running along the quay. These were used to carry stone to the pier for shipment to London.

After a time you come to a stone jetty where there are boats for hire. Turn right here and immediately right again into the High Street. The castellated tower rising from the rooftops on the left was once an astronomical observatory.

The High Street was the main street of old Swanage, and a handful of old buildings survive to indicate what the town was like before it became a holiday resort. The best of these is the White Swan, which stands on the left-hand side of the road close to the Square.

Carry straight on, passing the Anchor on the right, and the Red Lion on the left, and then turn right into Town Hall Lane. On the left, in a courtyard, is a lock-up or small prison with a very old door held together by iron nails. There was no-one inside it the last time I looked.

Swanage

Return to the High Street and turn right. The first building on the right is the Town Hall, one of many buildings that have earned Swanage the sobriquet of "Old London by the Sea". The three-storey central bay was brought from the Mercers' Hall in London, but its ornate carving looks rather out of place in a small seaside town.

On the other side of the road is Purbeck House, with its crow-stepped gables and castellated tower. The walls are covered with fragments of stone that were left over from the Albert Memorial. On the first floor of the tower are the initials of the owner, George Burt, and his motto "Know Thyself".

Beyond Purbeck House is a stretch of road where the pavement, walls and roofs are all made of Purbeck stone. On the right is a stone cross erected in 1909 on the site of the town pump. Turn right here into Church Hill. On the left is the Old Mill Pond that can be seen on all the postcards. This is where the village was that grew into the town of Swanage. Before the pump was erected the pond was the village water supply.

Follow the road round to the right. Through a gate on the right you can see the Tithe Barn, which is now a museum. Among the exhibits are an excellent model of the Isle of Purbeck and a collection of paintings of Purbeck manor houses. Admission is only 15p.

At the foot of the hill turn right into Kings Road. The Swan Brook flows along the side of the road between stone walls. The tiny round leaves of duckweed float on the water, and masses of pink-flowered valerian grow outwards from the walls. The road leads back to the mini-roundabout where the trail began.

POOLE

Location of the Start

Follow the signposts to the town centre, then follow the signposts to the "Old Town", and to the "Old Town multi-storey car park".

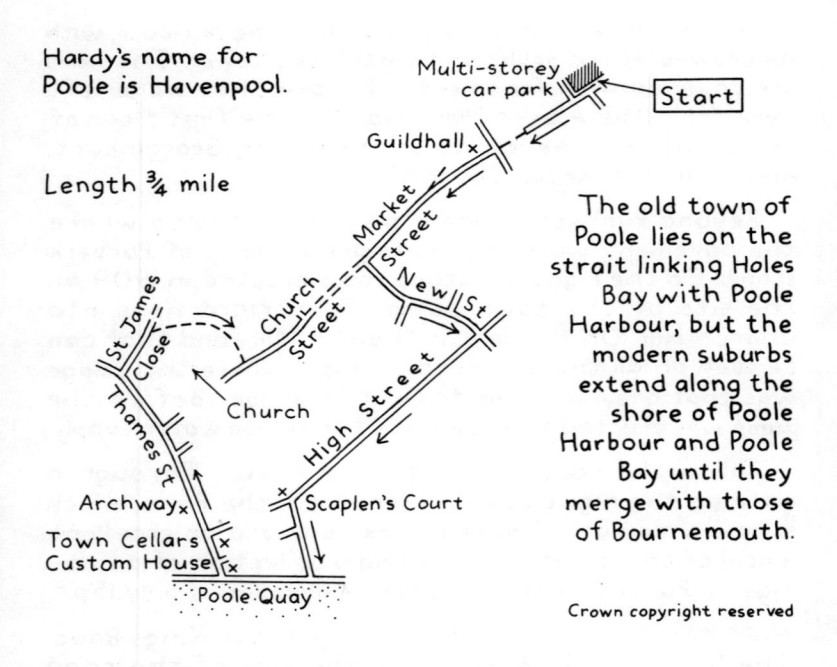

Hardy's name for Poole is Havenpool.

Length ¾ mile

The old town of Poole lies on the strait linking Holes Bay with Poole Harbour, but the modern suburbs extend along the shore of Poole Harbour and Poole Bay until they merge with those of Bournemouth.

Crown copyright reserved

On leaving the car park turn right. Keep straight on, crossing over New Orchard, and passing the eighteenth century Guildhall on the right. Turn left into New Street, and right into High Street. At the far end of the road on the right is Scaplen's Court, a fifteenth century house

Poole 51

which is now a museum. Turn left here, and right at the end of the road, into the Quay. This leads to the road junction illustrated below.

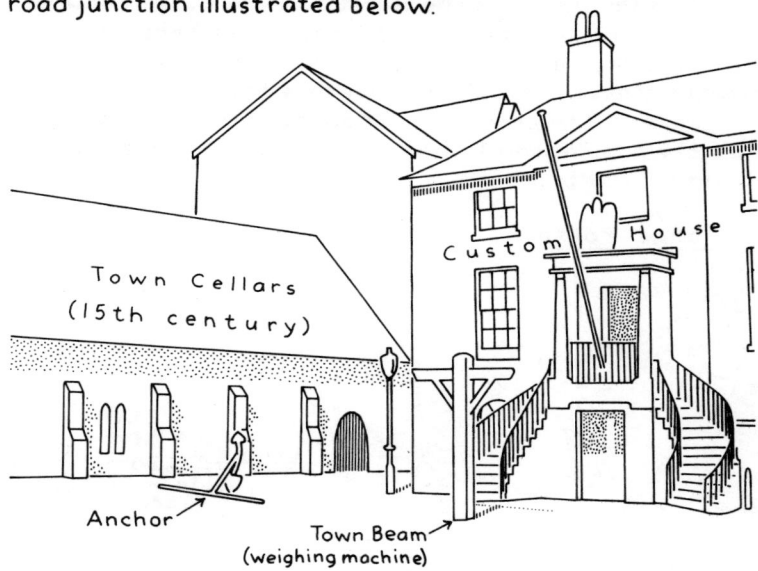

Town Cellars (15th century)

Custom House

Anchor

Town Beam (weighing machine)

Turn right here into Thames Street. Through an archway on the left you can see an old wall which is believed to be part of the Town Walls. The opening in it is the Water Gate.

At the far end of the churchyard turn right into St James Close, and then bear right onto a path which continues round the edge of the churchyard. At the end of the path turn left into Church Street. This is the most attractive street in the town, with modern houses in keeping with the old. It leads eventually back to the Guildhall, and so to the multi-storey car park.

BOURNEMOUTH

While Dorchester is the oldest town in Dorset, Bournemouth is the youngest. The first house here was built by Lewis Tregonwell in 1810, and later became the Royal Exeter Hotel. Now Bournemouth is the largest town in Dorset, and the centre of a conurbation that contains half the population of the county. Hardy's name for the town is Sandbourne.

(1) Longer route

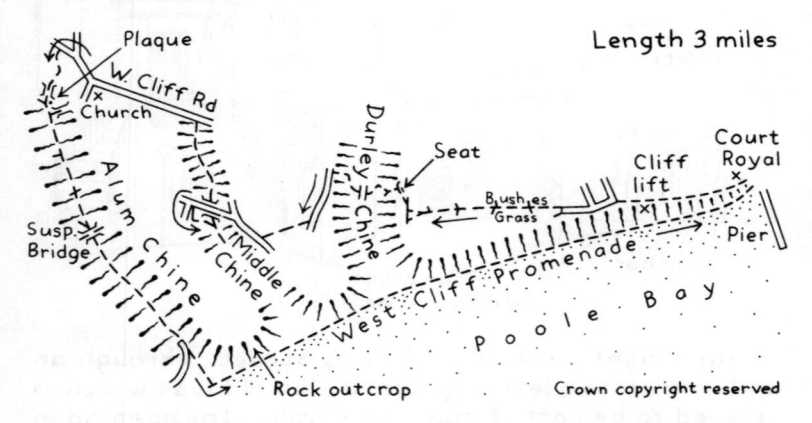

Length 3 miles

Crown copyright reserved

At the entrance to the pier, face the flyover and turn left along the top of the cliff. On the right is the Court Royal Convalescent Home for Mariners. In this building, in 1898, Guglielmo Marconi conducted experiments in wireless telegraphy that led to the invention of radio and television. Next to it is the Bournemouth International Centre, the principal conference centre in Britain, which was completed in 1984.

The slopes on the left are carpeted with wild

Bournemouth   53

flowers, including tamarisk, evening primroses, mallow and lupins. The only building on the left of the path is the terminal of the cliff lift, which might be regarded as a very steep railway, as it runs on rails. This is a good place to stop and study the view.

Looking east to the Isle of Wight

Hengistbury Head — Hurst Castle Lighthouse — Colwell Bay — Totland Bay — Brightstone Down (Continued below left)

Continued above right — Tennyson Down — Alum Bay — Needles Lighthouse — St Catherine's Down

Looking south-west to the Isle of Purbeck

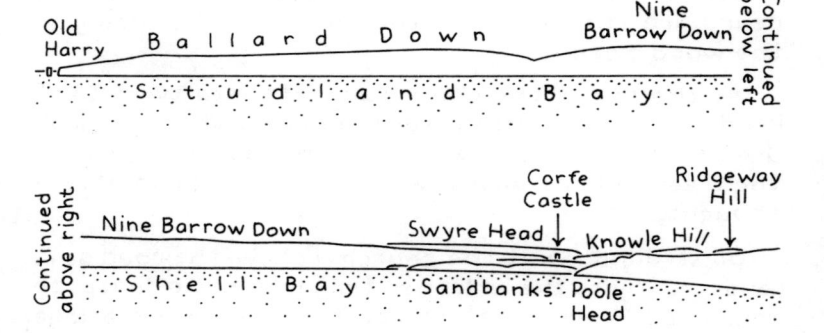

Old Harry — Ballard Down — Studland Bay — Nine Barrow Down (Continued below left)

Continued above right — Nine Barrow Down — Shell Bay — Swyre Head — Corfe Castle — Sandbanks — Poole Head — Knowle Hill — Ridgeway Hill

The enormous plants resembling cow parsley that are growing just past the lift terminal are giant hogweed.

After a quarter of a mile the path becomes a road. At the end of the road keep straight on, following the right hand edge of an area of grass. The path continues through scattered pines and rhododendrons, and eventually comes to a triangle of paths. Turn right here, and then immediately bear left. On the right is a wooden seat. The squirrels here are remarkably tame, and can sometimes be seen feeding from people's hands.

Turn left at the seat, down some steps, then bear right down more steps into Durley Chine. Cross over the road and continue up the other side to West Overcliff Drive. Open-decked buses run along here. Cross over the road and turn left. After passing number 10 on the right, turn right into a path called Cherry Tree Walk. At the end of the path turn right into West Overcliff Drive. Turn left over the bridge, and immediately left again down some steps. At the foot of the steps turn left, under the bridge, and follow a very attractive path through the rhododendrons of Middle Chine. The air smells sweet, and the only sounds to be heard are the singing of the birds and the cooing of the wood pigeons.

At the top of the chine turn left into West Cliff Road. This is a residential road, yet everywhere you look are trees. It is almost as though the road was built for the trees and the houses were only added as an afterthought.

Go straight on at the church. Follow the road as it bends slightly to the left, then turn left into a footpath signposted "Alum Chine". The path crosses over a bridge

Bournemouth

and meets another path. At the junction is a plaque recording the fact that Robert Louis Stevenson lived in a house overlooking this chine from 1884 to 1887. It was while he was here that he wrote "Kidnapped", and "The Strange Case of Dr Jekyll and Mr Hyde".

Bear left at the plaque, and follow the valley all the way down to the sea. Alum Chine is so called because alum was extracted from this area in the sixteenth century. In the eighteenth century wagon loads of brandy, tobacco, silk and lace were carried up the chine by smugglers. On the right is a side valley which has been made into a garden. Beyond the suspension bridge pine trees rise from the hillside and squirrels may be seen crossing from tree to tree.

Turn left along the sea front. High up on the cliff is a white rock formation. This is an outcrop of ball clay, which is used for making pottery. Just past it is a whole sequence of rock strata, with a dark brown stony layer at the top, then a steeper layer with vertical gullies, then a less steep area of darker sand, then a steeper area with horizontal layers close together, and so on down to the shore. These are the rocks of the heath, the Bagshot beds, named after Bagshot in Surrey where there is another area of heath.

On the way back to the pier you pass the entrances to two chines, Middle Chine, which is surprisingly rural in character, and Durley Chine, where there is another rock outcrop. Elsewhere the slopes are mostly covered in vegetation, the giant hogweed being very much in evidence. In the summer the sandy beach is crowded with people, and the sound of happy voices mingles with the sound of waves breaking on the shore. Occasionally you can see someone held high above the water by a parachute pulled by a boat.

(2) Shorter route

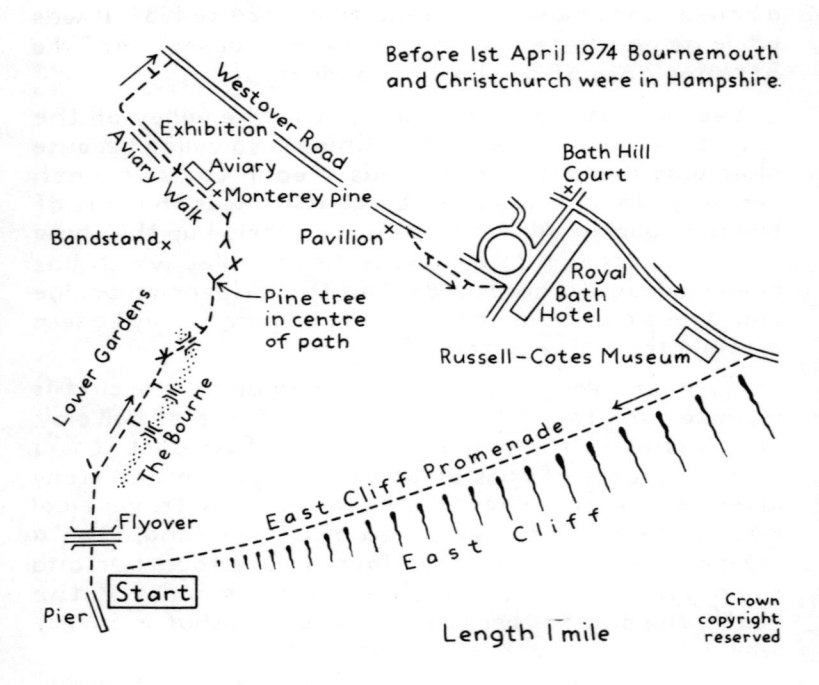

Before 1st April 1974 Bournemouth and Christchurch were in Hampshire.

Length 1 mile

Crown copyright reserved

From the entrance to the pier, pass under the flyover, keeping to the right of the island, and bear right along a path that runs parallel with the Bourne. This is the stream that gave Bournemouth its name. The path passes two bridges on the right, and then bears right over the stream. On the right are gardens of exceptional beauty, and in the summer you can usually hear music from the nearby bandstand.

When you come to a pine tree in the centre of the

Bournemouth

path turn right. Then turn left into a path that winds slightly between walls. On the left is a garden that commemorates Freddie Mills the boxer. Just past this turn left into Aviary Walk.

Immediately before the aviary is a pine tree whose needles are arranged in threes instead of the usual twos. This identifies it straight away as a Monterey pine. In the aviary are brightly-coloured birds from all over the world. They may be seen at any time, and there is no charge.

At the end of the aviary keep straight on. In the summer paintings are exhibited here on either side of the path. Above them the pine trees lean at crazy angles, and the music from the bandstand can still be heard.

After bending round to the right the path emerges from the park into Westover Road, the entertainment centre of Bournemouth. Turn right here. On the left is the A.B.C. Cinema, the Skating Rink and the Gaumont Cinema. On the right is the Pavilion Theatre. At the end of the Pavilion bear slightly right along a path which runs parallel with the road and comes out by a telephone box. Cross over the road to the entrance of the Royal Bath Hotel and turn left.

The Royal Bath Hotel is a really beautiful building, all crisp and white like the icing on a wedding cake. The building of this hotel in 1838 marks the beginning of Bournemouth as a holiday centre, for before that time the whole town consisted of just one house. In front of you the towers of Bath Hill Court rise from the trees, the pillars on the top floor giving them a slightly continental air. Altogether this is a most agreeable corner of Bournemouth.

At the end of the Royal Bath Hotel turn right into

Russell-Cotes Road. As you turn the corner, stop and look at the beautiful gardens at the foot of Bath Hill Court. Sometimes it seems as though Bournemouth is just one big garden.

At the top of the hill is the Russell-Cotes Museum. Outside are a number of exhibits including Bournemouth's first letter box. At the end of the museum turn sharp right. The view from here is similar to that depicted on page 53, but Durlston Head is now visible to the left of Old Harry, and Creechbarrow can be seen to the right of Ridgeway Hill.

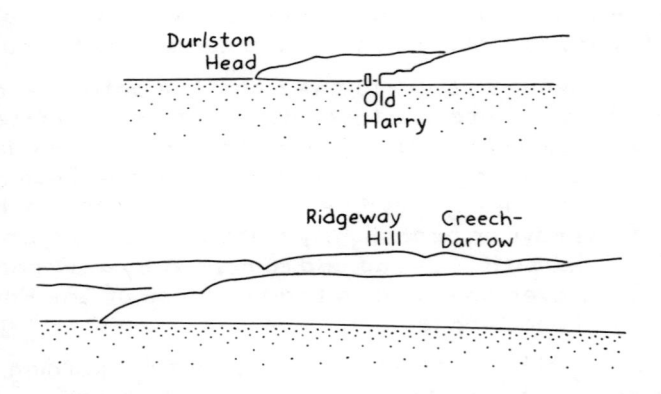

Carved in the wall on the right are the faces of Chaucer, Handel, Beethoven, Bacon, Scott and Shakespeare. Just past them is a collection of 200 specimens of rocks and fossils taken from different parts of the country. They are all identified in a catalogue obtainable in the museum.

From here the path leads back down to the pier, and more wild flowers can be seen on the left.

CHRISTCHURCH

Location of the start

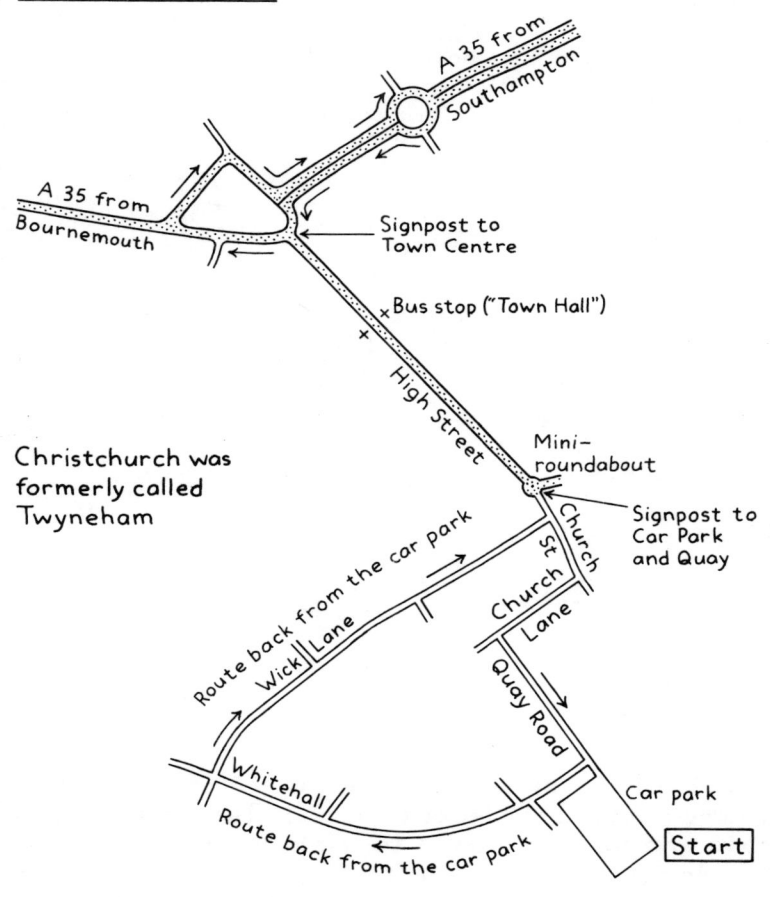

Christchurch was formerly called Twyneham

Crown copyright reserved

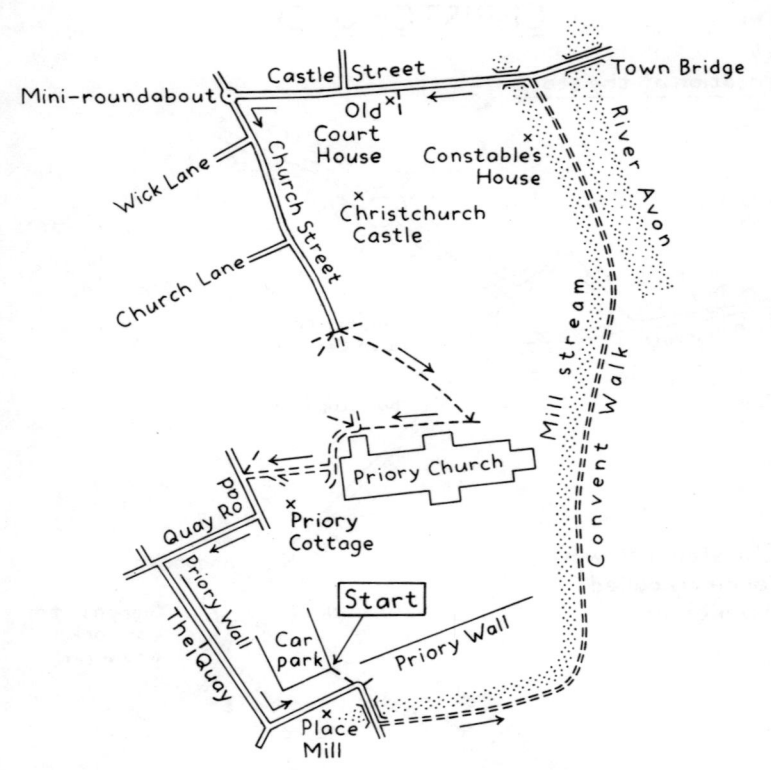

60   Christchurch

Length ¾ mile   Crown copyright reserved

Leave the car park by the far left-hand corner, where a short path leads to a road. Turn left into the road and follow it round to the right and over Place Mill Bridge. Then turn left onto an unmetalled road called Convent Walk, which runs along the side of the mill stream. Looking across the stream you can see

Christchurch

the ancient wall of the Priory precinct on the far side of the park.

The track goes round a left-hand bend and passes the end of the church. Farther on it follows a narrow strip of land between two rivers. This is rather like the Lynch at Lyme Regis but on a larger scale. The river on the right is the Avon, which flows through Salisbury.

From this strip of land you can see Christchurch Castle, the Constable's House and two lovely old bridges. The longer of the two, the Town Bridge, is a scheduled Ancient Monument.

The Castle was built in the thirteenth century on an artificial mound, or motte, that was raised in 1106. The Constable's House was built by the mill stream between 1160 and 1170. It is the oldest house in Dorset, and one of the oldest in Britain. There are two houses in Southampton and two more in Lincoln that are from this period, but it is not possible to date them accurately enough to say which is the oldest.

On the first floor, facing the stream, are two typical round-headed Norman windows. The first floor was the main floor of the house, the ground floor being used for storage. At the far end are the remains of a spiral staircase. The most notable feature of the building is a circular Norman chimney.

At the end of the track turn left into Castle Street. The first building on the left-hand side of the road is Old Court House. An inscription on the door proclaims that it was built in the twelfth century. The side wall, with its curved timbers, appears to be very old, but it is certainly not as old as this. Close to the side wall are the town stocks.

At the mini-roundabout, turn left into Church Street, and keep straight on into the cul-de-sac. There are two attractive Georgian houses on the left. At the end of the road bear left through a turnstile onto a path which goes diagonally across the churchyard. From here it is possible to appreciate the great length of the Priory Church. Apart from cathedrals, it is the longest church in England, and for this reason it is affectionately known as the Train.

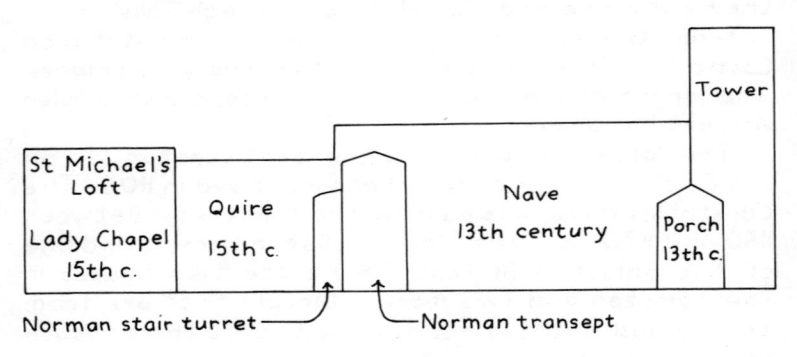

```
                                                          Tower
  ┌─────────────┬──────────┬───┬──────────────────┬──────┐
  │ St Michael's│          │   │                  │      │
  │    Loft     │  Quire   │   │     Nave         │ Porch│
  │ Lady Chapel │  15th c. │   │   13th century   │13th c│
  │   15th c.   │          │   │                  │      │
  └─────────────┴──────────┴───┴──────────────────┴──────┘
  Norman stair turret ──────┘   └── Norman transept
```

At the end of the path turn right along the side of the church, so that you can study its architecture more closely. The oldest features are the lower part of the North Transept and the adjoining stair turret, where there is a wealth of carved Norman stonework.

Christchurch Priory, more than any other building encountered on these trails, must be seen from the inside. You enter by a huge thirteenth century porch. Once inside, you can look left along the Nave and see the sunlight streaming in through the south windows of the Quire. Along the sides of the Nave are rows of massive Norman pillars and arches that are unsuspected from the outside. Above these are the smaller Norman arches of the Triforium. I usually prefer the architecture of houses to that of churches, but I must admit that the Constable's House has nothing to

Christchurch

compare with this.

From the porch, go round the corner to the front of the church, then bear right, passing a very old house called Priory Cottage on the left. When you reach the road turn left, then immediately right, then left into The Quay. On the left is a stretch of Saxon wall incorporating some brownish-purple stones.

The river that can be seen from here is the Stour, the second of the two great rivers that meet at Christchurch. At the end of the road turn left, passing on the right the historic Place Mill, which is open to the public in the summer.

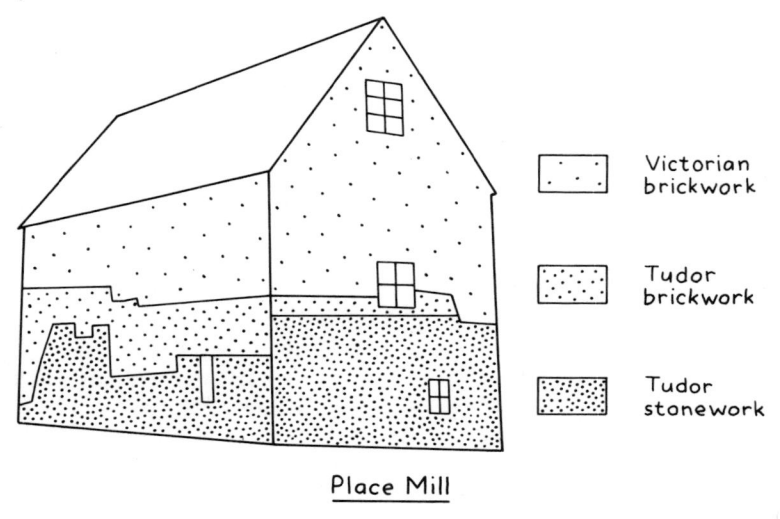

Victorian brickwork

Tudor brickwork

Tudor stonework

Place Mill

Just past the mill on the right is a millstone which is used as a table with seats round it. The grooves on the surface of the stone are called furrows and were used to grind the corn. The path back to the car park leaves the road opposite the bridge.